DESTINY AND STAR HUNTERS

Violent Fire Prayers to Reclaim your Original and Recover your Stolen Virtues & Potential in the Courts of Heaven

DESTINY AND STAR HUNTERS

Violent Fire Prayers to Reclaim your Original and Recover your Stolen Virtues & Potential in the Courts of Heaven

Prayer M. Madueke

PRAYER
PUBLICATIONS
UNITED STATES

Prayer M. Madueke

ISBN: 979-8850789480

Copyright © 2024 Prayer M. Madueke

Published by Prayer Publications.
Printed in the United States of America.

4 Free Ebooks

In order to say a 'Thank You' for purchasing *Destiny and Star Hunters*, I offer these books to you in appreciation. Click or type **madueke.com/free-gift** in your browser.

Message from the Author

I want to see you succeed, grow, and break free from negativity and obstacles. My hope is for you to thrive, unaffected by negative influences and challenging situations. Because of that, please permit me to introduce two courses that I believe passionately will help you:

1. To break the evil altars and powers of your father's house, The role of altars in the realm of existence is very key because altars are meeting places between the physical and the spiritual, between the visible and the invisible.

   Unless a man cuts off the evil flow from the power of his father's house, he will not fulfil his destiny. <u>Click here</u> to learn more about <u>my course</u> on how to tear down unholy altars and close the enemy's entryways into your life!

2. To help you seamlessly break iron-like problems, illness, delayed marriage, poverty, or any long-standing battle.

   Discover <u>the transformative power of Christian fasting and prayer</u>. Remember, Matthew 17:21 teaches us, *"But this kind of demon does not go out except by prayer and fasting."* Ready to overcome your struggles? <u>Click here</u> to learn more about this course.

Embrace the journey ahead with faith, for through prayer, fasting, and the dismantling of evil altars, you shall unlock the doors to spiritual liberation and divine breakthrough. May your path be illuminated by His grace as you walk towards a life free from bondage.

If you're seeing this from the physical copy, type the link: madueke.com/courses in your browser to view all the courses on my website.

Prayer
Madueke
CHRISTIAN AUTHOR

Christian Counselling

We were created for a greater purpose than only survival and God wants us to live a full life.

If you need prayer or counselling, or if you have any other inquiries, please visit the counselling page on my website to know when I will be available for a phone call.

Click or type links.madueke.com/counselling in your browser.

Let's Connect on Youtube ▶

Join me on my YouTube channel, "Prayer M. Madueke," where I share powerful insights, guidance, and prayers for spiritual breakthroughs.

Subscribe today to unlock the secrets of the Kingdom and embrace an abundant life. Let's grow together!

Click or type **links.madueke.com/youtube** in your browser.

TABLE OF CONTENTS

ONE

THE ORIGIN OF DESTINY AND STAR HUNTERS

S atan, who is also called Lucifer, the son of the morning, the devil, the adversary, the father of lies, the old serpent, the ruler of darkness, a sinner, a murderer and an accuser, is the source and the originator of destiny and star hunting.

> How art thou fallen from heaven, O Lucifer, son of the morning! how art thou cut down to the ground, which didst weaken the nations!
>
> — ISAIAH 14:12

When he was created, Satan had everything. He was handsome, rich and filled with wisdom. His creation was perfect. He was given a place in heaven and in the garden of Eden. But he was not satisfied (Ezekiel 28:11-18; Isaiah 14:12-20).

In spite of all the benefits he was enjoying, he started planning to overthrow God. He wanted to exalt himself above God. He got a third of the angels in heaven to connive with him in this evil plot. But before he could finish the execution of the plot, God threw him down from heaven to earth. His evil plan was cut short.

> Yet thou shalt be brought down to hell, to the sides of the pit.
>
> — ISAIAH 14:15

> And the angels which kept not their first estate, but left their own habitation, he hath reserved in everlasting chains under darkness unto the judgment of the great day
>
> Likewise also these filthy dreamers defile the flesh, despise dominion, and speak evil of dignities.
>
> — JUDE 1: 6, 8

Man was created with a powerful destiny and star. God handed the earth to him to rule over there. When Satan was chased down from heaven, he saw the beauty of the garden of Eden and he was not happy with man. He became envious of man. God made hell for Satan and his fallen angels where they will suffer eternally. So, you see. He had a lot of reasons not to be happy.

With other fallen angels, he vowed to make earth ungovernable for man. It has been a ferocious war ever since with man fighting Satan and his fallen angels. These fallen angels, who go by various sobriquets such as demons, principalities, evil powers, the rulers of the darkness of this world, spiritual wickedness in high places, liars, the gods of this world, the princes of the powers of the air, are locked in a supremacy battle with man.

(John 8:44; 2 Corinthians 4:4; Matthew 12:24; Ephesians 6:12).

Satan did not have that many powers before. It was his deception of man that promoted him. He went into the garden of Eden and deceived man (Genesis 3:1-8).

He stole the blessings that God gave to man: the dominion over all creation and power to control them (Genesis 1:27, 28; 2:19, 20).

He defiled the earth with his multitude of iniquities. He turned the Earth into the wilderness. He made cities desolate. He shocked the earth to its very foundations. He locked up man up in a prison of sin, sickness and oppression.

> Thou hast defiled thy sanctuaries by the multitude of thine iniquities, by the iniquity of thy traffick; therefore will I bring forth a fire from the midst of thee, it shall devour thee, and I will bring thee to ashes upon the earth in the sight of all them that behold thee.

> — EZEKIEL 28:18

> They that see thee shall narrowly look upon thee, and consider thee, saying, Is this the man that made the earth to tremble, that did shake kingdoms;

> That made the world as a wilderness, and destroyed the cities thereof; that opened not the house of his prisoners?

> — ISAIAH 14:16-17

This was how he introduced man to witchcraft, cultism and false religion. He taught man the evil of going after men with bright futures, men destined for greatness in order to steal their stars.

The story of Cain and Abel in the book of Genesis perfectly illustrates this. Abel rebelled against Satan by offering the right sacrifice to God. Satan got annoyed and possessed Cain. He made Cain go after the star and destiny of Abel. Unfortunately,

Abel failed to see the demon in Cain. Cain took Abel to an evil chamber. There, he tried to force Abel to join an evil cult. Abel refused to join Cain in practicing witchcraft, and he was killed.

Abel failed to exercise the power and dominion that God gave him in expelling the demon in Cain. He let Cain talk instead of passing a decree that would have arrested and incapacitated him. God had given Abel the power to rebuke demons but he failed to exercise it the way Jesus did again Peter.

> And Cain talked with Abel his brother: and it came to pass, when they were in the field, that Cain rose up against Abel his brother, and slew him.
>
> And out of the ground the Lord God formed every beast of the field, and every fowl of the air; and brought them unto Adam to see what he would call them: and whatsoever Adam called every living creature, that was the name thereof.
>
> And Adam gave names to all cattle, and to the fowl of the air, and to every beast of the field; but for Adam there was not found an help meet for him.
>
> — GENESIS 4:8; 2:19, 20

After Abel was killed, the devil recruited more men to go after the destinies and stars of people meant for greatness. He introduced idolatry and false religion. He became an intruder in the holy of holies, the church. He is the defiler of the holy altar He is the general overseer of disobedient priests. He is the uninvited monster in the house of God. He is the deceiver of old and young ministers. He is the killer of ordained ministers. He is the instigator of sorcery, witchcraft and magic. He sits upon the health, marriage and every business of man.

> And there came one of the seven angels which had the seven vials, and talked with me, saying unto me, Come hither; I will shew unto thee the judgment of the great whore that sitteth upon many waters.
>
> And he saith unto me, The waters which thou sawest, where the whore sitteth, are peoples, and multitudes, and nations, and tongues.
>
> — REVELATION 17:1, 15

The devil operates through agents who are very subtle and crafty. These agents are destiny and star hunters. They can deceive and spoil everything about you through evil dedication and idolatry. They afflict and oppress people with false doctrines. They release demons to torment and afflict people with false beliefs and evil practices. Their aim is to confuse people with the philosophy of men and vain deceit which contradicts Christ. They force people to follow the traditions of the world rather than Christ.

> Beware lest any man spoil you through philosophy and vain deceit, after the tradition of men, after the rudiments of the world, and not after Christ.
>
> — COLOSSIANS 2:8

The devil dealt man a devastating blow by deceiving and overthrowing him in the garden of Eden. Furthermore, the devil darkened man's understanding of God (Ephesians 4:18).

He made man's heart deceitful and desperately wicked (Jeremiah 17:9). The devil enslaved the will of man by defiling his mind and conscience and denying him spiritual understanding. He made man to go after the pleasures of this world instead of obeying the revealed will of God in the scriptures.

Christ came to save and show us the way. He came to tell us the truth and give us life (Matthew 11:28; John 14:6).

TWO

DESTINY AND STAR HUNTERS EXPOSED

B efore the coming of Christ, destiny and star hunters were busy spiritually plundering and destroying the earth. They controlled the world with occultism, witchcraft and sin. They attacked people with unrighteousness, fornication, wickedness, covetousness, envy, murder, deceit, malice, whispering, backbiting, hatred of God, pride, and boastfulness. The invention of evil things, disobedience to parents, lack of understanding, unfaithfulness, unnatural acts, evil desires, merciless and homosexual lifestyles became the order of the day just like today (Romans 1:28-31; Galatians 5:19-21).

They destroyed the family, the church and every branch of government.

> O God, why hast thou cast us off for ever? why doth thine anger smoke against the sheep of thy pasture?
>
> Remember thy congregation, which thou hast purchased of old; the rod of thine inheritance, which thou hast redeemed; this mount Zion, wherein thou hast dwelt.
>
> Lift up thy feet unto the perpetual desolations; even all that the enemy hath done wickedly in the sanctuary.
>
> — PSALMS 74:1-3

In the Old Testament, these destiny and star hunters formed occult groups. They turned people against God and stole their stars and destinies. People were forced to worship Satan. The elders and the ordained priests backslid and joined cults. They turned to the practice of witchcraft right inside the temple.

This is exactly what is happening in churches today. Most church gatherings today are gatherings of witches, wizards and occult groups.

We now have pastors and church leaders who are traitors, outcasts, captives, lepers, deceivers, high-level cultists, and destiny and star hunters. Their members suffer from all kinds of problems because God has forsaken them. With Their names removed from the book of Life, Satan freely attacks them. They become subject to the marks of hatred and rejection everywhere they go because the wrath of God is upon them. They become walking corpses, spiritually dead and empty. These unfortunate victims become exposed to demonic attacks, terror, shame, reproach, disgrace, and incurable diseases which make them wish for death (Exodus 32:33; Hebrews 3:19; 4:1; 10:38, 39; 1 Timothy 4:1, 2; Ezekiel 3:20; John 15:2, 6; Luke 9:62; 11:24-26).

> They have cast fire into thy sanctuary, they have defiled by casting down the dwelling place of thy name to the ground.
>
> — PSALMS 74:7

It began to look as if God has abandoned the world in anger. The destruction caused by destiny and star hunters seemed beyond human repair. These agents of destruction caused an increase in wickedness right inside the sanctuary of God. They're like lions in the midst of the congregation and persecuted the few remaining true believers. They changed the signs of God to ensigns. These occult grandmasters were promoted to positions of leadership in the church. They became rich and famous for hunting and wrecking people's stars and destinies. People under their control suffered terrible losses of fortune. Occult and witchcraft weapons, axes and hammers, both visible and invisible, were deployed against them. People with great destinies became subject to satanic oppression.

Satanic agents planted strange fires of sickness, barrenness, untimely deaths, late marriage, mental problems, incurable illnesses, just mention a few, in human organs, inside people's residence, offices and everywhere to monitor believers.

> They have cast fire into thy sanctuary, they have defiled by casting down the dwelling place of thy name to the ground.
>
> They said in their hearts, Let us destroy them together: they have burned up all the synagogues of God in the land.
>
> We see not our signs: there is no more any prophet: neither is there among us any that knoweth how long.
>
> — PSALMS 74:7-9

After spoiling the leadership of the world and defiling it, these satanic agents entered God's sanctuary, the Temple, in the Old

Testament. They defiled, polluted and inundated the congregation with intractable problems with no solutions in sight. Their goal was to destroy and close down the Temple and they nearly achieved these when the covid-19 Pandemic struck the world in late 2019- 2020.

Thanks be to God because in every generation there are always true worshippers who will rise to pray, intercede and remain pure.

> O God, why hast thou cast us off for ever? why doth thine anger smoke against the sheep of thy pasture?
>
> We see not our signs: there is no more any prophet: neither is there among us any that knoweth how long.
>
> — PSALMS 74:1, 9

Fortunately, the Old Testament believers did not give up. Even though the satanic agents in their midst bruised and battered them with attacks of barrenness, loneliness, isolation, the untimely death of their loved ones, sickness, shame, reproach and disgrace, they refused to give up or listen to the demands of the Cains of their generation.

They prayed for mercy and asked God to remember his congregation, which He purchased of old; the rod of his inheritance, which He redeemed. They asked God to come back to his deserted sanctuary and put a stop to the wickedness of destiny and star hunters. They asked him to silence the roaring and boasting of the evil church leaders (Ezekiel 8:1-18).

God clearly revealed to prophet Ezekiel the evil activities of these bad leaders.

> And he put forth the form of an hand, and took me by a lock of mine head; and the spirit lifted me up between the earth and the heaven, and brought me in the visions of God to Jerusalem, to the door of the inner gate that looketh toward the north; where was the seat of the image of jealousy, which provoketh to jealousy.
>
> He said furthermore unto me, Son of man, seest thou what they do? even the great abominations that the house of Israel committeth here, that I should go far off from my sanctuary? but turn thee yet again, and thou shalt see greater abominations.
>
> — EZEKIEL 8:3, 6

These astral travelers in Jerusalem worshiped images as personal gods in their houses and planted same at the gates of the house of God. They disobeyed God's commandments by worshipping and sacrificing to images (Exodus 20:3-5, 22, 23; 22:20; Leviticus 19:4; Deuteronomy 12:30, 31; 13:6-8; 17:2-5).

They served and feared other gods, worshiped angels and used images to worship the true God (Exodus 34:14-17; 23:13; Deuteronomy 4:15, 16, 19; 27:15; Romans 1:25-32).

> And there stood before them seventy men of the ancients of the house of Israel, and in the midst of them stood Jaazaniah the son of Shaphan, with every man his censer in his hand; and a thick cloud of incense went up.
>
> Then said he unto me, Son of man, hast thou seen what the ancients of the house of Israel do in the dark, every man in the chambers of his imagery? for they say, the Lord seeth us not; the Lord hath forsaken the earth.
>
> — EZEKIEL 8:11-12

When people embrace idolatry, God moves far away from them. This is especially so when people are led astray by fallen church leaders. This was what happened in Israel during the time of Ezekiel. Seventy men started secret evil cults. It had terrible repercussions.

If this happened in Israel, you can imagine the rot in places like Egypt or Babylon or our local communities. The evil sacrifices offered by these men in secret cults caused clouds of darkness to descend on the land (Numbers 23:1, 2, 13-14, 27-30).

It was a macabre competition with each evil cult trying to outdo the other in abominable things.

> And he brought me into the inner court of the Lord's house, and, behold, at the door of the temple of the Lord, between the porch and the altar, were about five and twenty men, with their backs toward the temple of the Lord, and their faces toward the east; and they worshipped the sun toward the east.
>
> Then he said unto me, Hast thou seen this, O son of man? Is it a light thing to the house of Judah that they commit the abominations which they commit here? for they have filled the land with violence, and have returned to provoke me to anger: and, lo, they put the branch to their nose.

> Therefore will I also deal in fury: mine eye shall not spare, neither will I have pity: and though they cry in mine ears with a loud voice, yet will I not hear them.

— EZEKIEL 8:16-18

Women wept to and worshiped their goddess, Tammuz in their evil cult while about 25 evil men boldly worshiped the sun god in defiance of the Almighty.

The evil activities of destiny and star hunters are behind the insecurity, violence, wars, incurable sickness, unnatural affects and strange manifestations of abominable sins all over the world. This is why God refuses to answer prayers. God is angry and his divine fury is heavy upon the nations of the earth. He does not answer the prayers of the wicked.

THREE

VICTIMS OF DESTINY AND STAR HUNTERS

During apostle Paul's missionary travels, he encountered a girl possessed with the spirit of divination. Star hunters were misusing this girl's star. This girl may have originally had the gift of prophecy. Star hunters trapped her and replaced her original gift with the divination (something God has vehemently warned His children against).

> And it came to pass, as we went to prayer, a certain damsel possessed with a spirit of divination met us, which brought her masters much gain by soothsaying:
>
> — ACTS 16:16

> They search out iniquities; they accomplish a diligent search: both the inward thought of every one of them, and the heart, is deep.
>
> — PSALMS 64:6

This spirit turned her away from God's divine purpose for her life. She became useless to her family, the community and her creator. The occult grandmasters controlling her were the ones exploiting her gift of divination to enrich themselves. She wasn't married and did not have children. In the eyes of society, she was useless. Even though she could see accurate visions sometimes, she had no capacity to solve people's problems, heal the sick or deliver the oppressed. All her efforts in life were misdirected into making her evil masters rich. She operated in direct contravention of God's word.

> A man was famous according as he had lifted up axes upon the thick trees. But now they break down the carved work thereof at once with axes and hammers.
>
> They have cast fire into thy sanctuary, they have defiled by casting down the dwelling place of thy name to the ground.
>
> — PSALMS 74:5-7

There are people feeding fat and growing rich on your suffering, hardship, sickness, poverty, and joblessness. An occult person in your family may be growing richer off your miseries. Your present ugly situation, late marriage, singlehood or inability to sustain good relationship with others may be fueling the evil prosperity of someone in your family.

The hostility and barrenness in your marriage or the stubbornness and uselessness of your children may be why evil people around you are prospering. Drug and alcohol abuse, waywardness and rebelliousness are symptoms of destinies hijacked by the wicked. The sad reality is that many have suffered to raise children only for those children to abandon them in their old age. This is not ordinary. It takes spiritual eye to discern the handwork of the wicked.

> Thy sons and thy daughters shall be given unto another people, and thine eyes shall look, and fail with longing for them all the day long; and there shall be no might in thine hand.
>
> Thou shalt beget sons and daughters, but thou shalt not enjoy them; for they shall go into captivity.
>
> — DEUTERONOMY 28:32, 41

Occult grandmasters hijack people's stars and cause parents to lose their children to wrong relationships and marriages. They can make you marry your enemy and ensure you always meet the wrong people in life. They spiritually capture the children of others and make sure the biological parents of such children never get to enjoy them. They attain great heights in society by offering occultic sacrifices.

They program sicknesses, spirits of madness and strange burning fires through evil dream to defile, and pollute the destinies of those greatly endowed to do exploit.

> Thou shalt betroth a wife, and another man shall lie with her: thou shalt build an house, and thou shalt not dwell therein: thou shalt plant a vineyard, and shalt not gather the grapes thereof.
>
> — DEUTERONOMY 28:30

> And the angels which kept not their first estate, but left their own habitation, he hath reserved in everlasting chains under darkness unto the judgment of the great day.

> Likewise also these filthy dreamers defile the flesh, despise dominion, and speak evil of dignities.

— JUDE 1: 6, 8

These star hijackers can transform into your spouse or a friend just to defile you with sex in a dream. They can afflict babies in the womb with sickness or deformity. Through witchcraft-inflicted dreams they can possess babies right inside the womb with anti-progressive demons. They offer evil sacrifices to reveal people's destinies which they waste with evil axes and occult hammers. They afflict, arrest and suppress people's stars. They get people initiated into the occult through evil sacrifices and subsequently destroy their marital life. Such people get into marriages with the wrong partners and this inevitably led to separation or divorce. Some may end up never getting married again.

The havocs they wreak are endless. They capture people's progress, joy, peace and destroy them. They place limitation, satanic embargos, full-stops to programs, projects and good relationships. They bury progressive stars, and mark victims with indelible signs of hatred and rejection everywhere they go. They close doors of opportunities and force victims to abandon good jobs and projects. They manipulate people into looking for help in wrong places.

In those days, while Mordecai sat in the king's gate, two of the king's chamberlains, Bigthan and Teresh, of those which kept the door, were wroth, and sought to lay hands on the king Ahasuerus.

And the thing was known to Mordecai, who told it unto Esther the queen; and Esther certified the king thereof in Mordecai's name.

And when inquisition was made of the matter, it was found out; therefore they were both hanged on a tree: and it was written in the book of the chronicles before the king.

After these things did king Ahasuerus promote Haman the son of Hammedatha the Agagite, and advanced him, and set his seat above all the princes that were with him.

— ESTHER 2:21-23; 3:1

They manipulate leadership selection and cause wrong decisions to be taken. The enemies of God are promoted into positions of authority. These wicked destroyers of destinies cause their victims to labor fruitlessly. They reap where they did not sow. They reward the wicked with undeserved promotions. They manipulate, confuse and change situations to favor their lackeys who may not have relevant qualifications.

And there was great joy in that city.

But there was a certain man, called Simon, which beforetime in the same city used sorcery, and bewitched the people of Samaria, giving out that himself was some great one:

To whom they all gave heed, from the least to the greatest, saying, This man is the great power of God.

And to him they had regard, because that of long time he had bewitched them with sorceries.

— ACTS 8:8-11

They can use sorcery to bewitch people, families, cities or nations. They can divert the efforts of people in a family or city to the enrichment of a single occult person while rendering others useless.

It is important to note that God never created anyone to be useless, unprofitable and unproductive. The implication is that even though you may not be useful to yourself, your family or your community, you are useful somewhere, making others rich. Your essence, your star is making someone rich.

FOUR

HOW CAN YOU BE DELIVERED?

T he truth is that there is no amount of devastation, damage or harm the devil can cause that cannot be restored perfectly by God. If God can heal the sick, cause dry bones to come together with lost flesh and raise the dead, there is nothing impossible before Him.

Shall the prey be taken from the mighty, or the lawful captive delivered?

But thus saith the Lord, Even the captives of the mighty shall be taken away, and the prey of the terrible shall be delivered: for I will contend with him that contendeth with thee, and I will save thy children.

And I will feed them that oppress thee with their own flesh; and they shall be drunken with their own blood,

as with sweet wine: and all flesh shall know that I the
Lord am thy Saviour and thy Redeemer, the mighty
One of Jacob.

— ISAIAH 49:24-26

Even if the devil swallowed you, he can be forced to vomit you, how much less human destiny and star hunters. For years, the occult grand masters kept the damsel of Thyatira in bondage with the spirit of divination. She suffered helplessly for years, enriching her masters but a simple prayer from Paul set her free. Paul pitied her suffering. He that her destiny has been denatured by these wicked men. This got him angry and he commanded the evil spirit of divination to depart from her. This restored the girl's star and destiny and rendered her useless to her evil masters.

And it came to pass, as we went to prayer, a certain damsel possessed with a spirit of divination met us, which brought her masters much gain by soothsaying:

The same followed Paul and us, and cried, saying, These men are the servants of the most high God, which shew unto us the way of salvation.

And this did she many days. But Paul, being grieved, turned and said to the spirit, I command thee in the

name of Jesus Christ to come out of her. And he came
out the same hour.

— ACTS 16:16-18

When the evil spirit in the damsel was cast out, her masters suffered grievous losses. Their containers sank at sea; their warehouses got burnt, and they must have had accidents. Red alerts must have appeared on their evil altars, and when they checked, they must have seen that their hope for evil gains were gone forever.

Immediately the spirit was cast out, containers, lorry loads, ships and aircrafts carrying the goods of the occult grand masters must have had accidents. Their factories, houses caught fire, many negative things, their warehouses burnt and there were negative reports of grievous deaths in the families of occult grand masters. There were red alerts in their evil altars and when they checked, they saw that the hopes of their gains were gone.

The spirit of divination returned to their evil altars and the original destiny, the star of the damsel, relocated her.

And when her masters saw that the hope of their gains was gone, they caught Paul and Silas, and drew them into the marketplace unto the rulers.

— ACTS 16:19;

But as one was felling a beam, the axe head fell into the water: and he cried, and said, Alas, master! for it was borrowed.

And the man of God said, Where fell it? And he shewed him the place. And he cut down a stick, and cast it in thither; and the iron did swim.

Therefore said he, Take it up to thee. And he put out his hand, and took it.

— 2 KINGS 6:5-7

If you acknowledge your sin, repent, confess and forsake them, your prayers will be answered. Your deliverance will take place and the evil spirits in you will be cast out. You will recover your losses and good things meant for you in the kingdom of darkness will return to you.

When you repent truly, and pray with enough-is-enough spirit, God's promises of deliverance will take place in your life.

> The wicked watcheth the righteous, and seeketh to slay him.
>
> The Lord will not leave him in his hand, nor condemn him when he is judged.
>
> — PSALMS 37:32, 33

Repentance will make you fit for Deliverance. It will make you qualified for the book of life. God promises to keep your star and destiny at the hands of evil-doers. He will bring to naught all evil decrees, utterances and satanic judgements against you. You will no longer be subject to condemnation and satanic bondage. Destiny and Star thieves will not see your back.

The voice of God will enter into every satanic prison, occult altar and witchcraft coven to rescue your destiny, star and glory.

> They search out iniquities; they accomplish a diligent search: both the inward thought of every one of them, and the heart, is deep.
>
> — PSALMS 64:6

> But the king commanded Jerahmeel the son of Hammelech, and Seraiah the son of Azriel, and Shelemiah the son of Abdeel, to take Baruch the scribe and Jeremiah the prophet: but the Lord hid them.
>
> — JEREMIAH 36:26

If you are serious with the prayers in this book, the commandments of destiny and star hunters will not be carried out in your life. Your case-file will no longer be available to evil forces. All satanic agents will avoid you because the mark of God will be placed upon your life.

God will hide you from all your enemies. They will look for you but will not find you no matter how hard they try.

> Now when Jesus was born in Bethlehem of Judaea in the days of Herod the king, behold, there came wise men from the east to Jerusalem,
>
> Saying, Where is he that is born King of the Jews? for we have seen his star in the east, and are come to worship him.
>
> When Herod the king had heard these things, he was troubled, and all Jerusalem with him.

And when he had gathered all the chief priests and scribes of the people together, he demanded of them where Christ should be born.

And they said unto him, In Bethlehem of Judaea: for thus it is written by the prophet,

And thou Bethlehem, in the land of Juda, art not the least among the princes of Juda: for out of thee shall come a Governor, that shall rule my people Israel.

Then Herod, when he had privily called the wise men, enquired of them diligently what time the star appeared.

— MATTHEW 2:1-7

Remember, when Jesus was born, God hid His star from Herod but revealed it to the Wise Men from the East. Though Herod tried to unravel it, God did not allow him to see the star of Jesus. Therefore, you need to truly repent, confess your sins, and forsake them and start praying without compromising.

There was in the days of Herod, the king of Judaea, a certain priest named Zacharias, of the course of Abia: and his wife was of the daughters of Aaron, and her name was Elisabeth.

> And they were both righteous before God, walking in all the commandments and ordinances of the Lord blameless.
>
> And they had no child, because that Elisabeth was barren, and they both were now well stricken in years.

— LUKE 1:5-7

Believers in the Old Testament such as Zechariah, Elizabeth, the Virgin Mary, Simeon and Hannah never gave up.

They confronted and conquered the destiny and star hunters of their time. They were probably among the believers that prayed in (Psalms 74:1-11).

Even though they suffered under the yoke of barrenness, Zechariah and Elizabeth persevered in serving God. They obeyed God without blaming anyone or anything for their misfortune. The yoke of barrenness which was brought upon them by destiny and star hunters followed them into old age but they never stopped living right.

Under the yoke of barrenness, Zechariah and Elizabeth, his wife served God, and lived a righteous life before God. They obeyed the commandments and were without blame. The yoke of barrenness fired against them by destiny and star killers persisted with them until old age but they never stopped living right. Zechariah served God as a priest and he was without blemish. He always burnt incense on the altar of the Most High at the right time and in the right way.

> And it came to pass, that while he executed the priest's office before God in the order of his course,
>
> According to the custom of the priest's office, his lot was to burn incense when he went into the temple of the Lord.
>
> And, behold, there was a man in Jerusalem, whose name was Simeon; and the same man was just and devout, waiting for the consolation of Israel: and the Holy Ghost was upon him.
>
> And it was revealed unto him by the Holy Ghost, that he should not see death, before he had seen the Lord's Christ.
>
> — LUKE 1:8, 9; 2:25, 26

Simeon was another example of a steadfast servant of God in the Old Testament. He defied the atrocious activities of destiny killers and hijackers and kept praying and waiting for the people of Israel to retrace their steps back to God. In the midst of a wicked generation, the Holy Ghost promised him that he will not see death until he has seen the Savior, Jesus Christ.

And he came by the Spirit into the temple: and when the parents brought in the child Jesus, to do for him after the custom of the law,

Then took he him up in his arms, and blessed God, and said,

Lord, now lettest thou thy servant depart in peace, according to thy word:

For mine eyes have seen thy salvation,

Which thou hast prepared before the face of all people;

A light to lighten the Gentiles, and the glory of thy people Israel.

— LUKE 2:27-32

The wicked and the reprobate tried to ensnare and kill him but they all failed. God preserved his life in the midst of the star destroyers. They attempted to manipulate him into sin but failed woefully. He remained just in this dealings and God kept him safe from the web of destiny and star hunters until his prayers were answered (Psalms 37:32, 33; 64:6; Jeremiah 36:26).

Simeon waited on the Lord in prayer. When others were committing fornication, living unrighteous lives, practicing wickedness, and breaking the covenants of God, he remained devout and prayerful. His prayers were all answered before he died. When Jesus was born, Simeon was the one who received Him into the temple. Even though he lived in the days of darkness, God permitted him to witness the light of salvation, the coming of Jesus Christ.

Are you going to die without deliverance, leaving your family, community, city in darkness without the light of Christ?

Anna, a prophetess, the daughter of Phanuel, of the tribe of Asher was of a great age in the days of Herod. When her fellow women were busy defiling themselves, she kept her virginity and lived holy.

> And there was one Anna, a prophetess, the daughter of Phanuel, of the tribe of Aser: she was of a great age, and had lived with an husband seven years from her virginity;
>
> And she was a widow of about fourscore and four years, which departed not from the temple, but served God with fastings and prayers night and day.
>
> And she coming in that instant gave thanks likewise unto the Lord, and spake of him to all them that looked for redemption in Jerusalem.
>
> — LUKE 2:36-38

Though destiny and star hunters killed her husband, she lived holy and just as a widow for eighty-four years. She was the quintessential example of a true widow, a rebuke to widows who defile their bodies for filthy lucre. How did she resist the advances of wealthy seducers, and wicked destiny and star hunters of her days? She made the decision to serve God in holiness and always spent time in the temple. She lived a life of fasting and prayer.

What are you using your day and night times for?

Hannah was not in a night club the day Jesus was presented in the temple. She was not caught in the sinful web of lesbianism, smoking, drinking and prostitution on that day. She was right there in the temple to offer her thanks to God for sending a savior to deliver mankind from the trap of sin. She was a loud witness for Christ.

God sent you on a ministry to your neighbors, family and friends, community, city and the nation. Have you fulfilled it? What is your decision regarding your salvation? Are you going to die in this situation without deliverance?

Many people are tied down by the evil powers of destiny and star hijackers. Others are living carnal lifestyles, enjoying worldly festivities and conversations. Many are consumed by the desire for immoral dressing and by worldly cares. Some are controlled by worldly pursuits and pleasures, demonic ambitions, and unprofitable enjoyment.

Will you allow worldliness and the love of the things of this world to deny you deliverance from destiny killers? God is calling you to rise above the lusts of the flesh and desire for the things of this world. Don't allow the lusts of your eyes and pride for sinful life ruin your relationship with God.

Simeon resisted destiny destroyers and star hunters and received full deliverance. Zechariah and Elizabeth did the same and their barrenness bowed to their faith. The Virgin Mary kept her body holy and fulfilled her destiny without defilement. You need to take a stand against the activities of destiny and star hunters of our time. This is the time to resist them and persistently pray for deliverance until something happens.

WARFARE SECTION

DECREES AGAINST DESTINY AND STAR HUNTERS [PART 1]

Almighty God, thank you beyond thank you for your deliverance power over my life, in the name of Jesus. I command the staff of the wicked over my life, destiny and star to be broken to pieces, in the name of Jesus. I break and loosen my destiny from the scepter of evil rulers assigned to waste my destiny, in the name of Jesus. Every enemy of my rest and peace of mind, body and spirit, be frustrated, in the name of Jesus. O Lord arise and deliver my destiny from every satanic captivity, in the name of Jesus.

How art thou fallen from heaven, O Lucifer, son of the morning! how art thou cut down to the ground, which didst weaken the nations!

For thou hast said in thine heart, I will ascend into heaven, I will exalt my throne above the stars of God: I will sit also upon the mount of the congregation, in the sides of the north:

I will ascend above the heights of the clouds; I will be like the Most High.

— ISAIAH 14:12-14

Every weapon of darkness hitting me from any side, I render you impotent, in the name of Jesus. Any evil throne holding me down in bondage, be dethroned, in the name of Jesus. Any evil voice speaking against my destiny, be silenced by the speaking blood of Jesus. I command the pomp of the wicked over my life to be brought down to the grave, in the name of Jesus.

Let the fall of the devil and his agents in my life be visibly noticed, in the name of Jesus. Every influence of Lucifer in my life, be terminated, in the name of Jesus. I command every evil kingdom that is attacking my life to be weakened, in the name of Jesus. Any evil thought against my destiny among the creatures, be frustrated, in the name of Jesus.

Yet thou shalt be brought down to hell, to the sides of the pit.

They that see thee shall narrowly look upon thee, and consider thee, saying, Is this the man that made the earth to tremble, that did shake kingdoms;

But thou art cast out of thy grave like an abominable branch, and as the raiment of those that are slain, thrust through with a sword, that go down to the stones of the pit; as a carcase trodden under feet.

— ISAIAH 14:15-16, 19

Let the sword of God cut off every demonic presence in every area of my life, in the name of Jesus. I command the congregation of the wicked against my life to scatter in shame and defeat, in the name of Jesus. Any demonic rise over my life, be destroyed and brought to nothing, in the name of Jesus.

Almighty God, by your power, I command every satanic kingdom against my life to tremble, shake and perish, in the name of Jesus. Any satanic prison, spiritually or physically, locking me up, open and release me by force, in the name of Jesus.

DECREES AGAINST DESTINY AND STAR HUNTERS [PART 2]

Let my deliverance bring endless lamentation in the kingdom of darkness forever, in the name of Jesus. Any evil king sitting in the throne of my life, be unseated without negotiation, in the name of Jesus. Any satanic seal against my destiny and star, be broken to pieces, in the name of Jesus.

Any evil force attacking my destiny from the sun, moon and stars, be crippled by the power of God, in the name of Jesus. I command the backbone of the devil and his agents over my life to be broken, in the name of Jesus. Let the protection of the devil and his agents over my life catch fire and burn to ashes, in the name of Jesus.

> Son of man, take up a lamentation upon the king of Tyrus, and say unto him, Thus saith the Lord God; Thou sealest up the sum, full of wisdom, and perfect in beauty.
>
> By the multitude of thy merchandise they have filled the midst of thee with violence, and thou hast sinned: therefore I will cast thee as profane out of the

mountain of God: and I will destroy thee, O covering cherub, from the midst of the stones of fire.

Thine heart was lifted up because of thy beauty, thou hast corrupted thy wisdom by reason of thy brightness: I will cast thee to the ground, I will lay thee before kings, that they may behold thee.

Thou hast defiled thy sanctuaries by the multitude of thine iniquities, by the iniquity of thy traffick; therefore will I bring forth a fire from the midst of thee, it shall devour thee, and I will bring thee to ashes upon the earth in the sight of all them that behold thee.

— EZEKIEL 28:12, 16-18

Almighty God, take away my destiny and star from every demonic captivity by your power, in the name of Jesus. Every demonic wisdom over my life, be turned to foolishness, in the name of Jesus. Any demonic investment in the garden of my life, be uprooted unto death, in the name of Jesus. Any evil mouth proudly speaking against me anywhere, be silenced unto death by the speaking blood of Jesus.

Ancient of days, deliver me from the powers of destiny and star hunters, in the name of Jesus. Any evil personality using my glory, destiny and star to prosper, be disgraced openly, in the name of Jesus. Father Lord, deliver me from the violence of destiny and star hunters, in the name of Jesus. Any evil heart lifted against my life, be cast down to destruction, in the name of Jesus. Any evil power assigned to corrupt and defile my destiny and star, I render you powerless, in the name of Jesus.

Blood of Jesus, enter into my foundation and cleanse the sanctuary of my destiny and star, in the name of Jesus. Every iniquity militating against my star and destiny, be destroyed by the speaking blood of Jesus. Let the devouring power of God devour every creature against my destiny and star, in the name of Jesus. Every enemy of my destiny and star, I bring you to ashes upon the earth, in the name of Jesus.

You, the demons pushed down from heaven with Lucifer, avoid me forever, in the name of Jesus. Every good thing I ever lost to the satanic kingdom in dreams, I recover you double, in the name of Jesus. Everything that ever happened to me in dreams from the satanic kingdom, receive destruction, in the name of Jesus.

I break and loosen myself from every evil dream covenant I ever entered into consciously or unconsciously, in the name of Jesus. I command every filthy dream assigned to waste my life to avoid me forever, in the name of Jesus. Blood of Jesus, deliver me from every defiled dream militating against my destiny and star, in the name of Jesus.

Father Lord, return my flesh the way you created it with your divine image and likeness, in the name of Jesus. Every sin in every area of my life, die by the speaking blood of Jesus. I receive back my dominion over the devil and his agents forever, in the name of Jesus. Any evil personality speaking evil against my destiny and star, be silenced unto death by the speaking blood of Jesus. Any demonic programme going on against my life, be terminated forever, in the name of Jesus.

DECREES AGAINST DESTINY AND STAR HUNTERS [PART 3]

Any agent of the devil in my family, neighborhood and anywhere that is assigned to waste my life, fail woefully, in the name of Jesus. Any problem in my life pushing me to join an evil group, receive an immediate solution, in the name of Jesus. Almighty God, increase your mercy and grace in my life to resist evil forces working against my destiny, in the name of Jesus.

Any evil personality working hard to initiate me against my faith in Christ, be frustrated, in the name of Jesus. Blood of Jesus, speak my destiny and my star out of the captivity of evil sacrifices, in the name of Jesus.

> And Cain talked with Abel his brother: and it came to pass, when they were in the field, that Cain rose up against Abel his brother, and slew him.
>
> And out of the ground the Lord God formed every beast of the field, and every fowl of the air; and brought them unto Adam to see what he would call them: and whatsoever Adam called every living creature, that was the name thereof.

> And Adam gave names to all cattle, and to the fowl of
> the air, and to every beast of the field; but for Adam
> there was not found an help meet for him.
>
> — GENESIS 4:8; 2:19, 20

I break and loosen myself forever from all relationships with the devil, in the name of Jesus. Every negative influence in my life from my Cain, I break away from you, in the name of Jesus. Any evil weapon the devil and his agents are using against my destiny and star, I render you impotent, in the name of Jesus.

I refuse to accept the will and plan of the devil and his agents over my life, in the name of Jesus. Almighty God, accept all my sacrifice and bless my destiny and star, in the name of Jesus. Any envious personality from anywhere working against my destiny and star, be exposed and disgraced, in the name of Jesus.

Every weapon of death working against my destiny and star, backfire, in the name of Jesus. Let my enemies use their weapons against themselves, in the name of Jesus.

> And there came one of the seven angels which had
> the seven vials, and talked with me, saying unto me,
> Come hither; I will shew unto thee the judgment of the
> great whore that sitteth upon many waters:

> And he saith unto me, The waters which thou sawest, where the whore sitteth, are peoples, and multitudes, and nations, and tongues.
>
> — REVELATION 17:1, 15

Father Lord, return me the way you created me with your full image and likeness, in the name of Jesus. Every yoke of darkness against my destiny and star, break into pieces, in the name of Jesus. Every corruption and defilement that ever took place in my life, be cleansed by the power in the blood of Jesus.

Almighty God, walk me out from every demonic field, camp and altars, in the name of Jesus. Any witchcraft animal living inside me, come out and die, in the name of Jesus. Every negative word ever spoken against my destiny and star, be converted to my favor, in the name of Jesus.

Any evil change assigned to waste my life, fail woefully, in the name of Jesus. I begin to unsay all that the devil and his agents ever said or will ever say against my destiny, in the name of Jesus. I command every creature to arise and defend the will of God in my life forever, in the name of Jesus.

Any power from any evil kingdom sitting upon my destiny, be unseated by death, in the name of Jesus. Any evil river/water flowing in any area of my life, dry up, in the name of Jesus. Any evil personality using my destiny to prosper, I command you to prosper no more, in the name of Jesus.

Almighty God, deliver me and my family from every dark kingdom, in the name of Jesus. Every problem in my life assigned to destroy me, receive destruction and avoid me forever, in the name of Jesus. Any mountain standing against my destiny, be removed forever, in the name of Jesus.

Every good thing my ancestors handed over to the devil and his agents, even from the days of Adam till now, I recover you double. You my blessings, glory in the camp of my enemies, return back to me now, in the name of Jesus. Any evil plan to dethrone God in my life, fail woefully, in the name of Jesus.

Every satanic delay in my life, be terminated, in the name of Jesus. Almighty God, bring me back fully to your plan and purpose, in the name of Jesus.

THANK YOU!

I'd like to use this time to thank you for purchasing my books and helping my ministry and work. Any copy of my book you buy helps to fund my ministry and family, as well as offering much-needed inspiration to keep writing. My family and I are very thankful, and we take your assistance very seriously.

You have already accomplished so much, but I would appreciate an honest review of some of my books through the link below. This is critical since reviews reflect how much an author's work is respected.

Please [click here] to leave a review on Amazon. If you're viewing from a printed version, please visit amazon.com/review/create-review?asin=B0C9SDN9DM to leave a review.

Please be aware that I read and value all comments and reviews. You can always post a review even though you haven't finished the book yet, and then edit your reviews later.

Thank you so much as you spare a precious moment of your time and may God bless you and meet you at the very point of your need.

You can also send me an email to hello@madueke.com if you encounter any difficulty while writing your review.

PRAYER M. MADUEKE'S BESTSELLING BOOKS

Click on any of the [Buy Now] buttons to view or purchase them on my website. If you're viewing from a printed version, please visit madueke.com and search for these books.

1.	Dictionary of Demons & Complete Deliverance	[Buy Now]
2.	Monitoring Spirits	[Buy Now]
3.	Praying with The Blood of Jesus	[Buy Now]
4.	The Power of Speaking in Tongues	[Buy Now]
5.	Speaking Things into Existence by Faith	[Buy Now]
6.	Discerning and Defeating the Ahab & Jezebel Spirit	[Buy Now]
7.	Defeating the Python Spirit	[Buy Now]
8.	35 Special Dangerous Decrees	[Buy Now]
9.	21/40 Nights of Decrees and Your Enemies Will Surrender	[Buy Now]

10. Command the Morning, Day and Night   [**Buy Now**]

11. Evil Summon   [**Buy Now**]

12. Overcoming & Destroying the Spirit of Rejection & Hatred   [**Buy Now**]

13. Queen of Heaven: Wife of Satan   [**Buy Now**]

14. The False Prophet   [**Buy Now**]

15. Dominion Over Sickness & Disease   [**Buy Now**]

16. The Battle Plan for Destroying Foundational Witchcraft   [**Buy Now**]

17. The Queen of the Coast   [**Buy Now**]

18. Dictionary of Unmerited Favor   [**Buy Now**]

19. Prayers for Breakthrough in your Business   [**Buy Now**]

20. A Jump From Evil Altar   [**Buy Now**]

21. 100 Days Prayers to Wake Up Your Lazarus   [**Buy Now**]

22. Breaking Evil Yokes   [**Buy Now**]

23. When Evil Altars are Multiplied   [**Buy Now**]

24. The Battle Plan for Destroying Foundational Occultism — [Buy Now]

25. Prayers for Protection — [Buy Now]

26. Prayers for Academic Success — [Buy Now]

27. Your Dream Directory — [Buy Now]

28. Prayers for Financial Breakthrough — [Buy Now]

29. Destiny and Star Hunters — [Buy Now]

30. Prayers to Pray during Courtship — [Buy Now]

31. 91 Days Decrees to Takeover the Year — [Buy Now]

32. Alone with God — [Buy Now]

33. Prayers against Satanic Oppression — [Buy Now]

34. Foundations Exposed — [Buy Now]

35. Prayers for Deliverance — [Buy Now]

36. Prayers to Heal Broken Relationship — [Buy Now]

37. Prayers for Good Health — [Buy Now]

38. Comprehensive Deliverance [**Buy Now**]

39. Prayers for College and University Students [**Buy Now**]

40. 40 Prayer Giants [**Buy Now**]

41. Divine Protection & Immunity While Sleeping [**Buy Now**]

42. Prayers for Fertility in your Marriage [**Buy Now**]

43. More Kingdoms to Conquer [**Buy Now**]

44. Confront and Conquer your Enemy [**Buy Now**]

45. Prayers to Raise Godly Children [**Buy Now**]

4 Free Ebooks

In order to say a 'Thank You' for purchasing *Destiny and Star Hunters*, I offer these books to you in appreciation. Click or type **madueke.com/free-gift** in your browser.

Message from the Author

I want to see you succeed, grow, and break free from negativity and obstacles. My hope is for you to thrive, unaffected by negative influences and challenging situations. Because of that, please permit me to introduce two courses that I believe passionately will help you:

1. To break the evil altars and powers of your father's house, The role of altars in the realm of existence is very key because altars are meeting places between the physical and the spiritual, between the visible and the invisible.

   Unless a man cuts off the evil flow from the power of his father's house, he will not fulfil his destiny. **Click here** to learn more about **my course** on how to tear down unholy altars and close the enemy's entryways into your life!

2. To help you seamlessly break iron-like problems, illness, delayed marriage, poverty, or any long-standing battle.

   Discover **the transformative power of Christian fasting and prayer**. Remember, Matthew 17:21 teaches us, *"But this kind of demon does not go out except by prayer and fasting."* Ready to overcome your struggles? **Click here** to learn more about this course.

Embrace the journey ahead with faith, for through prayer, fasting, and the dismantling of evil altars, you shall unlock the doors to spiritual liberation and divine breakthrough. May your path be illuminated by His grace as you walk towards a life free from bondage.

If you're seeing this from the physical copy, type the link: madueke.com/courses in your browser to view all the courses on my website.

Prayer
Madueke
CHRISTIAN AUTHOR

Christian Counselling

We were created for a greater purpose than only survival and God wants us to live a full life.

If you need prayer or counselling, or if you have any other inquiries, please visit the counselling page on my website to know when I will be available for a phone call.

Click or type **links.madueke.com/counselling** in your browser.

Let's Connect on Youtube ▶

Join me on my YouTube channel, "Prayer M. Madueke," where I share powerful insights, guidance, and prayers for spiritual breakthroughs.

Subscribe today to unlock the secrets of the Kingdom and embrace an abundant life. Let's grow together!

Click or type **links.madueke.com/youtube** in your browser.

An Invitation to Become a Ministry Partner

I appreciate the support and inquiries I have received regarding collaboration with my ministry. Your prayers and dedication to the work of the Kingdom are highly valued.

You can also visit the donation page on my website if you would like to contribute or learn more about supporting my ministry: **madueke.com/donate**.

Thank you for your continued support and faithfulness in Christ Jesus.

www.ingramcontent.com/pod-product-compliance
Lightning Source LLC
Chambersburg PA
CBHW031234120626
46545CB00003B/1111